40 DAYS
TO
A NEW
BEGINNING

A Fasting and Prayer Guide for Spiritual Transformation and Renewal

THE
CORNERSTONE
P U B L I S H I N G

YEMI E. AJIMATANRAREJE

40 DAYS TO A NEW BEGINNING
A Fasting and Prayer Guide for Spiritual Transformation and Renewal

Copyright © 2017 by Yemi E. Ajimatanrareje
ISBN: 978-1-944652-49-4

Cornerstone Publishing
A Division of Cornerstone Creativity Group LLC
Phone: +1(516) 547-4999
info@thecornerstonepublishers.com
www.thecornerstonepublishers.com

To order bulk of this book or to contact the author please:
call 1 (925) 481-4936 or Email: Yemaji@aol.com
www.openheavenscommunitychurch.org
Address: 3933A Walnut Blvd. Brentwood, CA 94513

DEDICATION

I dedicate this book to God Almighty, who saved my life from destruction and brought me into His marvelous light.

His calling upon my life to preach the gospel has given me joy and real fulfillment! Conversely, it also brought me face-to-face with untold hardships, trials and tribulations. This led me to start praying and fasting the way I never did. And that was what led to the birth of this book, *40 Days to A New Beginning*.

Soli Deo Gloria - Glory to God Alone!

ACKNOWLEDGMENTS

I wish to acknowledge the great contributions of my wife, Dr. Rose Ajimatanrareje, to the birth of this book. She actually wrote some of the prayers and kept encouraging me to write until the manuscript was completed.

I am also thankful to our daughter, Ayoyemi, who offered some helpful suggestions after she read the summary of the book.

My gratitude goes to all those who had worked with me in ministry and made me see the need to write this prayer guide.

May God bless you all.

Dr. Yemi E. Ajimatanrareje
Brentwood, California

INTRODUCTION

This 40-Day Fasting & Prayer guide is a spiritual compass that will help you navigate the waters as you decide to fast and pray for 40 days. It provides you with day-to-day guidance, regarding Scripture readings, written prayers and space to write messages you receive from God. Set your faith loose. Set your face on God. Set yourself apart for God and He will indeed do a new thing in your life! You are about to start receiving all the NEW THINGS He has in store for you.

Hear what God says in Isaiah 43:19 (NKJV) "Behold, I will do a new thing, Now it shall spring forth; Shall you not know it? I will even make a road in the wilderness And rivers in the desert."

This prophetic utterance applies to you and your life, just as it applied to the Israelites in Babylonian captivity during the time of Prophet

Isaiah. The Israelites received deliverance, restoration and a new covenant. The Lord is set, too, to give you deliverance, restoration, strength and spiritual transformation.

I pray that as you begin your own fast, every embargo placed on your progress is henceforth lifted in the name of Jesus. I decree that every obstacle on your road to success is permanently removed by a divine fiat!

- Heavens shall open up over your life and all your operations in the name of Jesus.
- Your star must rise and begin to shine brightly according to God's will.
- Your life shall be filled with signs and wonders as you are made for signs and wonders (Isaiah 8:18).

I prophesy that this 40-day fasting and prayers you are about to embark on will mark the beginning of unprecedented spiritual transformation and renewal in your life. It shall be your stepping stone to total victory, breakthroughs and extraordinary miracles in all areas of your life in the name of Jesus.

The stagnation, failure, frustration, oppression,

suppression, demotion, depression, poverty, barrenness, sickness, unemployment, unending struggles and sufferings you may have experienced must come to an end in the name of Jesus.

You deserve to start living life and living it more abundantly. Jesus states in John 10:10 (NKJV) that: "...I have come that they may have life, and that they may have it more abundantly.

It is time for a total turn around for the best in your life. Your season of new blessings, new favor and new breakthroughs is here. This is a 40-day journey to help you break new grounds in an extraordinary manner. Your time to excel and be celebrated has come. Draw nearer to God and receive the fullness of His promises, His plan and purpose for your life.

Once you begin the fast by faith, you will need to spend time with God daily by studying the Holy Bible, praying fervently in preparation for your astonishing miracles!

Jesus fasted for forty days and forty nights. When the tempter came to tempt Him, Jesus prevailed and drove the tempter away. In fact, angels came to Jesus immediately after to attend to Him (Matthew 4:1-11). He then began His ministry with signs and wonders.

Elijah fasted for forty days and forty nights. He travelled to Mount Horeb, and there God appeared to him and spoke to him (1 Kings 19:8-9).

Rain fell on the earth for forty days and forty nights (Genesis 7:12) to clean out sin and corruption. Thereafter, a new dispensation, pioneered by Noah and his family, came about.

God is going to look upon your 40-day fasting and prayers with favor; and give you newness on all fronts. He will give you beauty for ashes, joy instead of mourning, success for failure, fulfillment instead of frustration and a garment of praise instead of a spirit of despair.

A divine visitation replete with new anointing, new garment, new power, guidance and success is about to take place in your life and it will surely last a lifetime in the name of Jesus.

FORMAT OF THE 40-DAY FASTING & PRAYERS

1. Abstain from eating food, snacks and drinking of beverages from 6AM-3PM each day of the 40 days. You may drink water during and after the specified time of your fast.

2. Study your Bible everyday. Meditate on the Word you have read and pray the prayers suggested below for each day.

3. Plan to pray for about 30 minutes at 12MIDNIGHT (Acts 16:25). Include Psalm 35 in your Scripture reading as you pray."

Day 1
REPENT & REQUEST GOD'S POWER

Scripture Reading: 2 Chronicles 7:13-16

13 When I shut up heaven and there is no rain, or command the locusts to devour the land, or send pestilence among My people, 14 if My people who are called by My name will humble themselves, and pray and seek My face, and turn from their wicked ways, then I will hear from heaven, and will forgive their sin and heal their land. 15 Now My eyes will be open and My ears attentive to prayer made in this place. 16 For now I have chosen and sanctified this house, that My name may be there forever; and My eyes and My heart will be there perpetually.

For further reading: Psalms 51

PRAYERS

1. I thank you Lord for allowing me to participate in this 40-day fasting and prayers. Strengthen and empower me to do it faithfully to the very end in Jesus' name.

2. I declare in the name of Jesus that my prayers and fasting shall not be in vain in the name of Jesus.

3. Lord, I humble myself and repent from all my sins. Forgive me and wash me clean from all unrighteousness in the name of Jesus.

4. I plead the blood of Jesus upon every organ of my body for cleansing and purification in the name of Jesus.

5. Lord, I claim the new things you are doing in my life during this season in the name of Jesus.

*Notes*_____

_____

_____

_____

_____

Day 2
BREAKING DOWN EVIL GATES
AND ANCIENT DOORS

Scripture: Psalms 24:3-9

3 Who may ascend into the hill of the Lord?
Or who may stand in His holy place?
4 He who has clean hands and a pure heart,
Who has not lifted up his soul to an idol,
Nor sworn deceitfully.
5 He shall receive blessing from the Lord,
And righteousness from the God of his salvation.
6 This is Jacob, the generation of those who seek Him,
Who seek Your face. Selah
7 Lift up your heads, O you gates!
And be lifted up, you everlasting doors!
And the King of glory shall come in.
8 Who is this King of glory?
The Lord strong and mighty,
The Lord mighty in battle.
9 Lift up your heads, O you gates!
Lift up, you everlasting doors!
And the King of glory shall come in.

PRAYERS

1. I decree that every evil gate and dark cloud hanging over my life, be lifted and destroyed permanently in the name of Jesus.
2. I use the full armor of God to break down every ancient door shut against my success in the name of Jesus.
3. Whoever is holding on to my blessings, I command you to release them immediately in the name of Jesus.
4. O Lord, let total destruction come upon the ancient serpent tormenting my life in the name of Jesus.
5. I command every obstacle and obstruction in my path to disappear immediately in the name of Jesus.
6. Lord, open unto me every great door that the enemy has closed in the name of Jesus.

*Notes*_____

_____

_____

_____

_____

Day 3
BREAK THE YOKE OF SATANIC OPPOSITION

Scripture: Psalms 35:1-28.

1 Plead my cause, O Lord, with those who strive with me;

Fight against those who fight against me.

2 Take hold of shield and buckler,

And stand up for my help.

3 Also draw out the spear,

And stop those who pursue me.

Say to my soul,

"I am your salvation."

4 Let those be put to shame and brought to dishonor

Who seek after my life;

Let those be turned back and brought to confusion

Who plot my hurt.

5 Let them be like chaff before the wind,

And let the angel of the Lord chase them.

6 Let their way be dark and slippery,

And let the angel of the Lord pursue them.

Continue to Verses 7-28

PRAYERS

1. Every evil seed growing in my life, be uprooted by fire in the name of Jesus.
2. Every spiritual storm of poverty plaguing my life, be silenced now in the name of Jesus.
3. O God! Let the alliance of my enemies be confused and completely destroyed in the name of Jesus.
4. Let every valley of death and suffering assigned against my life turn into blessings and victory for me in the name of Jesus.
5. Heavenly Father, let them be afraid and brought to confusion all who rejoice at my downfall in the name of Jesus.
6. O God! Let the blood of Jesus blot out every opposition working against my life in the name of Jesus.

*Notes*_____

_____

_____

_____

_____

Day 4
FREEDOM FROM
OPPRESSION

Scripture: Isaiah 58:1-4

1 "Cry aloud, spare not;
Lift up your voice like a trumpet;
Tell My people their transgression,
And the house of Jacob their sins.
2 Yet they seek Me daily,
And delight to know My ways,
As a nation that did righteousness,
And did not forsake the ordinance of their God.
They ask of Me the ordinances of justice;
They take delight in approaching God.
3 'Why have we fasted,' they say, 'and You have not
seen? Why have we afflicted our souls, and You take
no notice?' "In fact, in the day of your fast you find
pleasure, and exploit all your laborers.
4 Indeed you fast for strife and debate,
And to strike with the fist of wickedness.
You will not fast as you do this day,
To make your voice heard on high.

Continue to Verses 5-14

PRAYERS

1. I destroy every barrier placed on my road to success in the name of Jesus.
2. Lord, loose the chains of injustice operating in my life in the name of Jesus.
3. Father, break into pieces every yoke of oppression, suppression and depression in my life in the name of Jesus.
4. I decree and declare that I am set free from every power limiting my progress and breakthroughs in the name of Jesus.
5. Lord, let my light break forth like the dawn and allow my healing to come quickly to me in the name of Jesus.
6. Father, help me to seek you with a sincere heart everyday.
7. Lord, let my desires be pure and pleasing in your sight in the name of Jesus.

*Notes*_____

_____

_____

_____

_____

Day 5
O LORD, REVIVE ME

Scripture: Joel 2:28-30

28 "And it shall come to pass afterward
That I will pour out My Spirit on all flesh;
Your sons and your daughters shall prophesy,
Your old men shall dream dreams,
Your young men shall see visions.
29 And also on My menservants and on My
maidservants
I will pour out My Spirit in those days.
30 "And I will show wonders in the heavens and in the
earth: Blood and fire and pillars of smoke.

For further reading: Acts 2:1-4

PRAYERS

1. Father, revive my soul, spirit and body in the name of Jesus.
2. Lord, pour out your Spirit on all flesh in the land on which I live in the name of Jesus.
3. Fire of the Holy Spirit, come afresh into my life and empower me to do the extraordinary and achieve the supernatural in the name of Jesus.
4. Lord, anoint me to speak in new tongues and also have the gift of interpretation in the name of Jesus
5. Heavenly Father, cause your fire of revival to be ignited in every true Church all over our land in the name of Jesus.
6. Lord, give me the desire to pray continually until I receive answers to my prayers in Jesus' name.

*Notes*_____

_____

_____

_____

_____

Day 6
TOTAL VICTORY IS MINE

Scripture: Psalms 36:1-12

1 An oracle within my heart concerning the transgression
of the wicked:
There is no fear of God before his eyes.
2 For he flatters himself in his own eyes,
When he finds out his iniquity and when he hates.
3 The words of his mouth are wickedness and deceit;
He has ceased to be wise and to do good.
4 He devises wickedness on his bed;
He sets himself in a way that is not good;
He does not abhor evil.
5 Your mercy, O Lord, is in the heavens;
Your faithfulness reaches to the clouds.
6 Your righteousness is like the great mountains;
Your judgments are a great deep;
O Lord, You preserve man and beast.

Continue to Verse 7-12

PRAYERS

1. Lord, let all the wickedness targeted against me backfire in the name of Jesus.
2. Father, preserve my life from untimely death in the name of Jesus.
3. Lord, let your river of delight flow through my heart everyday in the name of Jesus.
4. King of glory, let me find refuge in the shadow of your wings in the name of Jesus.
5. I declare that every satanic agent sent to attack me shall lie fallen, thrown down and unable to rise in the name of Jesus.
6. Lord, I declare that I am a victor everyday not a victim in the name of Jesus.
7. I decree and declare that I am victorious in all my dreams in Jesus' name.

*Notes*_____

_____

_____

_____

_____

_____

Day 7
LEAD ME, O LORD

Scripture: Psalms 1

1Blessed is the man
Who walks not in the counsel of the ungodly,
* Nor stands in the path of sinners,*
* Nor sits in the seat of the scornful;*
2 But his delight is in the law of the Lord,
* And in His law he meditates day and night.*
3 He shall be like a tree
* Planted by the rivers of water,*
* That brings forth its fruit in its season,*
* Whose leaf also shall not wither;*
And whatever he does shall prosper.
4 The ungodly are not so,
But are like the chaff which the wind drives away.
5 Therefore the ungodly shall not stand in the judgment,
Nor sinners in the congregation of the righteous.
6 For the Lord knows the way of the righteous,
But the way of the ungodly shall perish.

PRAYER

1. Lord, let Jesus increase in my life and in the lives of all that are associated with me in the name of Jesus.
2. Father, let your living water quench the thirst for sins and worldly pleasures in my life in the name of Jesus.
3. O Lord, wake me up from all manner of spiritual slumber in the name of Jesus.
4. Father, renew my mind with your mighty power and enable me to be discerning.
5. Lord, take your place in my life completely and lead me in the path of righteousness everyday in the name of Jesus.

*Notes*_____

_____

_____

_____

_____

_____

_____

_____

Day 8
LORD, HEAL ME

Scripture: James 5:13-17

13 Is anyone among you suffering? Let him pray. Is anyone cheerful? Let him sing Psalms. 14 Is anyone among you sick? Let him call for the elders of the church, and let them pray over him, anointing him with oil in the name of the Lord. 15 And the prayer of faith will save the sick, and the Lord will raise him up. And if he has committed sins, he will be forgiven. 16 Confess your trespasses to one another, and pray for one another, that you may be healed. The effective, fervent prayer of a righteous man avails much. 17 Elijah was a man with a nature like ours, and he prayed earnestly that it would not rain; and it did not rain on the land for three years and six months.

PRAYERS

1. Lord, I declare that I am healed in the name of Jesus.
2. I confess that my body is the temple of the Holy Spirit and it is free from every disease and infirmity in the name of Jesus.
3. O Lord, let every symptom of terminal illness in my life disappear immediately in the name of Jesus.
4. I use the shield of faith to extinguish all flaming arrows of the evil one shot at me in the name of Jesus.
5. I decree that my healing is permanent in the name of Jesus.

*Notes*_____

_____

_____

_____

_____

_____

_____

Day 9
DELIVERANCE FROM DEMONIC POSSESSION

Scripture: Mark 9:23-29

23 Jesus said to him, "If you can believe, all things are possible to him who believes."

24 Immediately the father of the child cried out and said with tears, "Lord, I believe; help my unbelief!"

25 When Jesus saw that the people came running together, He rebuked the unclean spirit, saying to it: "Deaf and dumb spirit, I command you, come out of him and enter him no more!" 26 Then the spirit cried out, convulsed him greatly, and came out of him. And he became as one dead, so that many said, "He is dead." 27 But Jesus took him by the hand and lifted him up, and he arose.

28 And when He had come into the house, His disciples asked Him privately, "Why could we not cast it out?" 29 So He said to them, "This kind can come out by nothing but prayer and fasting."

PRAYERS

1. Lord, deliver me from every strange and curious activity in the name of Jesus.
2. I renounce every association with Satan and the kingdom of darkness in the name of Jesus.
3. I uproot and tear down every evil plant and stronghold in my life in the name of Jesus.
4. I plead the blood of Jesus over my life for complete deliverance and restoration in the name of Jesus.
5. Satan! Loosen your hold upon my life permanently in the name of Jesus.

*Notes*_____

_____

_____

_____

_____

_____

_____

_____

Day 10
O YOU HEAVENS, FAVOR ME

Scripture: Psalms 8:1-6

O Lord, our Lord,

How excellent is Your name in all the earth,

Who have set Your glory above the heavens!

2 Out of the mouth of babes and nursing infants

You have ordained strength,

Because of Your enemies,

That You may silence the enemy and the avenger.

3 When I consider Your heavens, the work of Your fingers,

The moon and the stars, which You have ordained,

4 What is man that You are mindful of him,

And the son of man that You visit him?

5 For You have made him a little lower than the angels,

And You have crowned him with glory and honor.

6 You have made him to have dominion over the works of Your hands;

You have put all things under his feet,

PRAYERS

1. Lord, I pray for open heavens today and everyday of my life in the name of Jesus.

2. I decree and I declare that you, sun, moon and stars, favor me everyday you come forth in the name of Jesus.

3. Every evil spiritual force in the heavenly realm working against my life, be destroyed and thrown down in the name of Jesus.

4. I decree that every negative thing written in the cycle of the sun and moon against my life be blotted out in the name of Jesus.

5. O Lord, let every battle raging against me anywhere be won in my favor in the name of Jesus.

6. Father, release your angels to bear me up in their hands daily for maximum protection in Jesus' name.

*Notes*_____

_____

_____

_____

Day 11
THE BLESSINGS OF OBEDIENCE ARE MINE

Scripture: Deuteronomy 28: 1-14

"Now it shall come to pass, if you diligently obey the voice of the Lord your God, to observe carefully all His commandments which I command you today, that the Lord your God will set you high above all nations of the earth. 2 And all these blessings shall come upon you and overtake you, because you obey the voice of the Lord your God:

3 "Blessed shall you be in the city, and blessed shall you be in the country.

4 "Blessed shall be the fruit of your body, the produce of your ground and the increase of your herds, the increase of your cattle and the offspring of your flocks.

5 "Blessed shall be your basket and your kneading bowl.

6 "Blessed shall you be when you come in, and blessed shall you be when you go out.

Continue to verses 7-14

PRAYERS

1. All the blessings God has willed for my life, come upon me, and overtake me even as I obey the Lord in all things in the name of Jesus

2. Blessings of the city and country in which I live, come to me and my family in the name of Jesus

3. You the fruit of my womb, be blessed, and again I say be blessed in the name of Jesus.

4. O Lord, release your blessings in abundance on the work of my hands.

5. O Lord, establish me and my family as a holy people to Yourself in the name of Jesus.

6. Father, teach me to obey you in every area of my life in the name of Jesus.

*Notes*_____

_____

_____

_____

_____

Day 12
BLOOD OF JESUS, SPEAK FOR ME

Scriptures: Hebrews 12: 22-24

22 But you have come to Mount Zion and to the city of the living God, the heavenly Jerusalem, to an innumerable company of angels, 23 to the general assembly and church of the firstborn who are registered in heaven, to God the Judge of all, to the spirits of just men made perfect, 24 to Jesus the Mediator of the new covenant, and to the blood of sprinkling that speaks better things than that of Abel.

For further reading: Revelation 12:7-12

PRAYERS

1. Blood of Jesus, the Lamb that was slain, speak salvation into the life of _____ (mention the name) in the name of Jesus.

2. Blood of Jesus, speak victory for me in the name of Jesus.

3. Blood of Jesus, speak defeat for my enemies in the name of Jesus.

4. Blood of Jesus, speak prosperity for me and my loved ones in the name of Jesus.

5. Blood of Jesus, speak in my life every single moment in the name of Jesus

6. Blood of Jesus, bring about my divine exchange today in the name of Jesus.

7. Blood of Jesus, blot out every handwriting of the enemy working against my life in the name of Jesus.

*Notes*_____

_____

_____

_____

_____

Day 13
AFFLICTION WILL NOT RISE UP A SECOND TIME

Scripture: Nahum 1:12-13

12 Thus says the Lord:
"Though they are safe, and likewise many,
Yet in this manner they will be cut down
When he passes through.
Though I have afflicted you,
I will afflict you no more;
13 For now I will break off his yoke from you,
And burst your bonds apart."

For further reading: Isaiah 49:24-26

PRAYERS

1. Thank you Lord for your mercies and compassion; may my life not be afflicted any more in the name of Jesus.

2. O Lord, break off all yokes from off my neck in the name of Jesus

3. O Lord, burst any bonds of captivity in my life in Jesus' name.

4. Poverty shall not arise again in my life in the name of Jesus.

5. The wicked shall no more oppress me in the name of Jesus.

6. Father, let all my oppressors eat their own flesh and drink their own blood and be drunk as with sweet wine in the name of Jesus.

7. Lord, give me the discernment and wisdom to avoid mistakes of the past in Jesus' name.

*Notes*_____

_____

_____

_____

_____

Day 14
BLESS THE LORD, O MY SOUL

Scripture: Psalms 103: 1-5

Bless the Lord, O my soul;
And all that is within me, bless His holy name!
2 Bless the Lord, O my soul,
And forget not all His benefits:
3 Who forgives all your iniquities,
Who heals all your diseases,
4 Who redeems your life from destruction,
Who crowns you with lovingkindness and tender mercies,
5 Who satisfies your mouth with good things,
So that your youth is renewed like the eagle's.

PRAYERS

1. O Lord, I thank you for all Your benefits
2. O Lord, I ask forgiveness for all my sins (mention them here).
3. I am healed from _____(mention the disease or condition here) by the stripes on the body of Jesus.
4. O Lord, redeem my life from that which would destroy me in the name of Jesus.
5. O Lord, crown me with your love, joy, tender mercies and satisfy my mouth with good things.

*Notes*_____

_____

_____

_____

_____

_____

_____

_____

Day 15
O GOD DEFEND ME

Scripture: Psalms 20:1-7

May the Lord answer you in the day of trouble;
May the name of the God of Jacob defend you;
2 May He send you help from the sanctuary,
And strengthen you out of Zion;
3 May He remember all your offerings,
And accept your burnt sacrifice. Selah
4 May He grant you according to your heart's desire,
And fulfill all your purpose.
5 We will rejoice in your salvation,
And in the name of our God we will set up our banners!
May the Lord fulfill all your petitions.
6 Now I know that the Lord saves His anointed;
He will answer him from His holy heaven
With the saving strength of His right hand.
7 Some trust in chariots, and some in horses;
But we will remember the name of the Lord our God.

PRAYERS

1. O Lord, answer me in my day of trouble.
2. My helpers from the throne of God, locate me by the guidance of the Holy Spirit in the name of Jesus.
3. O Lord, remember all my offerings and sacrifices.
4. Father, grant me the desires of my heart.
5. O Lord, fulfill all my petitions.
6. Lord, I commit all my plans into your hands, grant me success as I execute them.
7. As I place my trust in you Lord, Let me be rewarded mightily in the name of Jesus.

*Notes*_____

_____

_____

_____

_____

_____

_____

_____

Day 16
O LORD HEAR ME

Scripture: Malachi 3:16-18

16 Then those who feared the Lord spoke to one another,
And the Lord listened and heard them;
So a book of remembrance was written before Him
For those who fear the Lord
And who meditate on His name.
17 "They shall be Mine," says the Lord of hosts,
"On the day that I make them My jewels.[a]
And I will spare them
As a man spares his own son who serves him."
18 Then you shall again discern
Between the righteous and the wicked,
Between one who serves God
And one who does not serve Him.

PRAYERS

1. O Lord, let a book of remembrance be opened before you for me and my loved ones who fear you and meditate on your name.
2. Spare me from calamity in the name of Jesus.
3. Father, fulfill your purpose in my life.
4. O Lord, answer me from Your holy heaven with the saving strength of Your right hand.
5. Heavenly Father, answer me when I call.
6. Lord, hearken to all my cries for mercy and help me to overcome every difficulty in my life in the name of Jesus.

*Notes*_____

_____

_____

_____

_____

_____

_____

Day 17
O GOD, EMPOWER ME

Scripture: Genesis 49:22-25

22 "Joseph is a fruitful bough,
A fruitful bough by a well;
His branches run over the wall.
23 The archers have bitterly grieved him,
Shot at him and hated him.
24 But his bow remained in strength,
And the arms of his hands were made strong
By the hands of the Mighty God of Jacob
(From there is the Shepherd, the Stone of Israel),
25 By the God of your father who will help you,
And by the Almighty who will bless you
With blessings of heaven above,
Blessings of the deep that lies beneath,
Blessings of the breasts and of the womb.

PRAYERS

1. Father, make my hand strong and blessed in the name of Jesus.
2. O Lord, bless me with blessings of heaven above in the name of Jesus.
3. Almighty God, bless me with blessings of the waters in the name of Jesus.
4. O God my Father, bless me with blessings of the finest treasure in the land on which I live in the name of Jesus.
5. O Father, let blessings up to the utmost, abound everyday in my life in the name of Jesus.

*Notes*_____

_____

_____

_____

_____

_____

_____

Day 18
O LORD, TEACH ME TO PRAY

Scripture: Matthew 6:6-13

6 But you, when you pray, go into your room, and when you have shut your door, pray to your Father who is in the secret place; and your Father who sees in secret will reward you openly.

7 And when you pray, do not use vain repetitions as the heathen do. For they think that they will be heard for their many words. 8 "Therefore do not be like them. For your Father knows the things you have need of before you ask Him. 9 In this manner, therefore, pray: Our Father in heaven, Hallowed be Your name. 10 Your kingdom come. Your will be done on earth as it is in heaven. 11 Give us this day our daily bread.

12 And forgive us our debts,

As we forgive our debtors.

13 And do not lead us into temptation,

But deliver us from the evil one.

For Yours is the kingdom and the power and the glory forever. Amen.

PRAYERS

1. Father, inspire me to praise your name all the day long.
2. O Lord, let your kingdom come and be fully established over all the earth in Jesus' name.
3. O Lord, let your will be done in my life.
4. Holy Spirit, teach me your Word in the name of Jesus.
5. O Lord, forgive me my sins and lead me to live a life of holiness.
6. Father, teach me to pray only with the leading of the Holy Spirit.
7. Fill my prayers Lord with fire and power in the name of Jesus.

*Notes*_____

_____

_____

_____

_____

_____

_____

Day 19
O GOD, PROTECT ME

Scripture: Isaiah 43

But now, thus says the Lord, who created you, O Jacob,
And He who formed you, O Israel:
"Fear not, for I have redeemed you;
I have called you by your name;
You are Mine.
2 When you pass through the waters, I will be with you;
And through the rivers, they shall not overflow you.
When you walk through the fire, you shall not be burned,
Nor shall the flame scorch you.
3 For I am the Lord your God,
The Holy One of Israel, your Savior;
I gave Egypt for your ransom,
Ethiopia and Seba in your place.

Continue to verses 4-28

PRAYERS

1. O Lord, do not let the waters of life overwhelm me.
2. The fire of life shall not burn me in the name of Jesus.
3. The flame of life shall not scorch my loved ones and I in the name of Jesus.
4. O God, make a roadway in the wilderness for me in the name of Jesus.
5. O Lord, make streams in the desert for me.

*Notes*_____

_____

_____

_____

_____

_____

_____

_____

_____

Day 20
THE VISION OF GOD FOR MY
LIFE, MANIFEST BY FIRE

Scripture: Habakkuk 2:2-4

2 Then the Lord answered me and said:
Write the vision
And make it plain on tablets,
That he may run who reads it.
3 For the vision is yet for an appointed time;
But at the end it will speak, and it will not lie.
Though it tarries, wait for it;
Because it will surely come,
It will not tarry.
4 "Behold the proud,
His soul is not upright in him;
But the just shall live by his faith.

PRAYERS

1. I will run with the vision God has given me by the power of the Holy Spirit in the name of Jesus.
2. O God, accelerate the appointed time of the fulfillment of Your vision for my life in the name of Jesus.
3. O Lord, help me to wait patiently on you
4. I cancel all demonic delays in my life with the blood of Jesus.
5. I shall live by faith and not by sight in the name of Jesus.

*Notes*_____

_____

_____

_____

_____

_____

_____

_____

_____

Day 21
O GOD DELIVER US

Scripture: Acts 12:11-15

11 And when Peter had come to himself, he said, "Now I know for certain that the Lord has sent His angel, and has delivered me from the hand of Herod and from all the expectation of the Jewish people." 12 So, when he had considered this, he came to the house of Mary, the mother of John whose surname was Mark, where many were gathered together praying. 13 And as Peter knocked at the door of the gate, a girl named Rhoda came to answer. 14 When she recognized Peter's voice, because of her gladness she did not open the gate, but ran in and announced that Peter stood before the gate. 15 But they said to her, "You are beside yourself!" Yet she kept insisting that it was so. So they said, "It is his angel."

PRAYERS

1. O Lord, send Your angels to rescue my loved ones and I from every Herod operating in our lives in the name of Jesus.
2. Cause them to fly swiftly to our aid in the name of Jesus.
3. May my divine helpers locate me by the fire of the Holy Spirit in the name of Jesus.
4. All satanic guards and policemen of darkness on assignment against my life, be put to death now in the name of Jesus.
5. May all the expectations of my enemies regarding my destiny be cut off in the name of Jesus.
6. O Lord, set free all those who are wrongfully held captive in the name of Jesus.
7. I break loose from every captivity of Satan, the world and the flesh in Jesus' name.

*Notes*_____

_____

_____

_____

_____

Day 22
O MY GOD, RESTORE ME

Scripture: Joel 2:25-27

*"So I will restore to you the years that the swarming
locust has eaten,*
The crawling locust,
The consuming locust,
And the chewing locust,[a]
My great army which I sent among you.
26 You shall eat in plenty and be satisfied,
And praise the name of the Lord your God,
Who has dealt wondrously with you;
And My people shall never be put to shame.
*27 Then you shall know that I am in the midst of
Israel:*
I am the Lord your God
And there is no other.
My people shall never be put to shame.

PRAYERS

1. O Lord, restore unto me all the years that the locust has eaten in the name of Jesus.
2. Father, restore unto me double of all that I have lost in the name of Jesus.
3. O Lord, cause the former rain and the latter rain to come down for me in the name of Jesus.
4. I decree and declare that I am walking in an overflow of oil in the name of Jesus.
5. O my soul, praise the name of the Lord your God, rejoice and be glad in the name of Jesus.

*Notes*_____

_____

_____

_____

_____

_____

_____

_____

Day 23
I WILL DO YOUR WILL, O LORD

Scripture: Johnah 2:1-10

Then Johnah prayed to the Lord his God from the fish's belly. 2 And he said:
"I cried out to the Lord because of my affliction,
And He answered me.
"Out of the belly of Sheol I cried,
And You heard my voice.
3 For You cast me into the deep,
Into the heart of the seas,
And the floods surrounded me;
All Your billows and Your waves passed over me.
4 Then I said, 'I have been cast out of Your sight;
Yet I will look again toward Your holy temple.'
5 The waters surrounded me, even to my soul;
The deep closed around me;
Weeds were wrapped around my head.

Continue from verses 6-10

PRAYERS

1. O Lord, let your will be accomplished in my life everyday.
2. I refuse to board any ship of disobedience in the name of Jesus.
3. O Lord, cause any fish holding me captive as a result of disobedience to vomit me now as I obey you in the name of Jesus.
4. Heavenly Father, help me to be an obedient child of God in the name of Jesus.
5. I declare that I shall not die but live to declare the works of the Lord in the name of Jesus.

*Notes*_____

_____

_____

_____

_____

_____

_____

_____

Day 24
I WILL SERVE YOU ONLY, O GOD

Scripture: Daniel 3:1-25

Nebuchadnezzar the king made an image of gold, whose height was sixty cubits and its width six cubits. He set it up in the plain of Dura, in the province of Babylon. 2 And King Nebuchadnezzar sent word to gather together the satraps, the administrators, the governors, the counselors, the treasurers, the judges, the magistrates, and all the officials of the provinces, to come to the dedication of the image which King Nebuchadnezzar had set up. 3 So the satraps, the administrators, the governors, the counselors, the treasurers, the judges, the magistrates, and all the officials of the provinces gathered together for the dedication of the image that King Nebuchadnezzar had set up; and they stood before the image that Nebuchadnezzar had set up.

Continue to verses 4-25
For further reading: Daniel 6:1-28.

PRAYERS

1. O Lord, help me to serve you no matter what in the name of Jesus.
2. In the order of Meshach, Shadrach and Abednego, be with me and my loved ones in any fire of life in the name of Jesus.
3. In the order of Daniel, O Lord, shut the mouth of any lion in my life in the name of Jesus.
4. I shall be celebrated in the presence of kings in the name of Jesus.
5. I declare that people will indeed praise God in my life in the name of Jesus.

*Notes*_____

_____

_____

_____

_____

_____

Day 25
THE WORD OF GOD IS POWERFUL

Scripture: Daniel 6:1-2

1 It pleased Darius to set over the kingdom one hundred and twenty satraps, to be over the whole kingdom; 2 and over these, three governors, of whom Daniel was one, that the satraps might give account to them, so that the king would suffer no loss.

For further reading: Daniel 3:1-25

PRAYERS

1. Sword of the Spirit, cut into pieces any power sitting on my star in the name of Jesus.
2. I decree and I declare that I am an overcomer by the blood of the lamb and the word of my testimony in the name of Jesus.
3. As I meditate on God's word day and night, I pray therefore that I have good success in the name of Jesus.
4. I declare O Lord, that Your Word is a lamp unto my feet and a light unto my path in the name of Jesus.
5. I pray that I shall live by every word that proceeds from the mouth of God in the name of Jesus.

*Notes*_____

_____

_____

_____

_____

_____

Day 26
THE NAME OF THE LORD IS A STRONG TOWER

Scripture: Mark 16:17-18

17 And these signs will follow those who believe: In My name they will cast out demons; they will speak with new tongues; 18 they will take up serpents; and if they drink anything deadly, it will by no means hurt them; they will lay hands on the sick, and they will recover."

PRAYERS

1. Every knee of infirmity in my life, bow at the mention of the name of Jesus.
2. I bind and cast out every demonic spirit that is stealing from me in the name of Jesus.
3. Lord, fill me with boldness and anointing as I speak your Word to unbelievers around me in the name of Jesus.
4. I declare that as I lay hands on the sick they recover immediately in the name of Jesus.
5. Father, teach me to hide myself in You in the name of Jesus.

*Notes*_____

_____

_____

_____

_____

_____

_____

Day 27
CONTEND O LORD WITH THOSE WHO CONTEND WITH ME

Scripture: Psalms 35

Plead my cause, O Lord, with those who strive with me;
Fight against those who fight against me.
2 Take hold of shield and buckler,
And stand up for my help.
3 Also draw out the spear,
And stop those who pursue me.
Say to my soul,
"I am your salvation."
4 Let those be put to shame and brought to dishonor
Who seek after my life;
Let those be turned back and brought to confusion
Who plot my hurt.
5 Let them be like chaff before the wind,
And let the angel of the Lord chase them.

Continue to verses 6-28

PRAYERS

1. O Lord, fight against those who fight against me in the name of Jesus.
2. O Lord, expose and put to shame those who seek after my life in the name of Jesus
3. Father, send your angel to pursue my pursuer in the name of Jesus.
4. King of glory, do not let my enemies rejoice over me in the name of Jesus.
5. O Lord, give me an astounding testimony in the name of Jesus.

*Notes*_____

_____

_____

_____

_____

_____

_____

_____

_____

Day 28
MY DREAMS MUST PROSPER ME

Scripture: Genesis 37:5-11

5 Now Joseph had a dream, and he told it to his brothers; and they hated him even more. 6 So he said to them, "Please hear this dream which I have dreamed: 7 There we were, binding sheaves in the field. Then behold, my sheaf arose and also stood upright; and indeed your sheaves stood all around and bowed down to my sheaf."

8 And his brothers said to him, "Shall you indeed reign over us? Or shall you indeed have dominion over us?" So they hated him even more for his dreams and for his words.

9 Then he dreamed still another dream and told it to his brothers, and said, "Look, I have dreamed another dream. And this time, the sun, the moon, and the eleven stars bowed down to me."

Continue to verses 10-11

PRAYERS

1. I declare that I will dream dreams from the throne room of God in the name of Jesus.
2. Dreams given me by God, manifest by fire in the name of Jesus.
3. Any evil dream I have ever had will never see the light of day in the name of Jesus.
4. Holy Spirit, interpret my dreams for me in the name of Jesus.
5. In the order of Joseph, let my dreams of prosperity, promotion and prominence come to pass in the name of Jesus.
6. I pray that the hands of the Lord shall be upon me continually in Jesus' name.
7. Father, let your abiding presence be with all Christians going through persecution in the name of Jesus.

*Notes*_____

_____

_____

_____

_____

Day 29
I SHALL DWELL IN THE SECRET PLACE OF THE MOST HIGH

Scripture: Psalms 91:1-6

*He who dwells in the secret place of the Most High
Shall abide under the shadow of the Almighty.
2 I will say of the Lord, "He is my refuge and my
fortress; My God, in Him I will trust."
3 Surely He shall deliver you from the snare of the
fowler And from the perilous pestilence.
4 He shall cover you with His feathers,
And under His wings you shall take refuge;
His truth shall be your shield and buckler.
5 You shall not be afraid of the terror by night,
Nor of the arrow that flies by day,
6 Nor of the pestilence that walks in darkness,
Nor of the destruction that lays waste at noonday.*

Continue to verses 7-16

PRAYERS

1. Father, I pray that You'll make my home a place of prayer in the name of Jesus.
2. The Most High is our dwelling place therefore, no evil shall befall my loved ones and I in the name of Jesus.
3. Lord, as we have set our eyes and love upon You, deliver me and my family from tragedy and trials in the name of Jesus.
4. I declare that God will set us on high because we have known His name in the name of Jesus.
5. Father, honor and satisfy every true believer with long life in the name of Jesus.

*Notes*_____

_____

_____

_____

_____

_____

_____

Day 30
I WILL ENTER HIS GATES
WITH THANKSGIVING

Scripture: Psalms 100

1 Make a joyful shout to the Lord, all you lands!
2 Serve the Lord with gladness;
Come before His presence with singing.
3 Know that the Lord, He is God;
It is He who has made us, and not we ourselves;[a]
We are His people and the sheep of His pasture.
4 Enter into His gates with thanksgiving,
And into His courts with praise.
Be thankful to Him, and bless His name.
5 For the Lord is good;
His mercy is everlasting,
And His truth endures to all generations.

For further reading: Psalms 136

PRAYERS

1. I thank You O Lord for the strength you gave me to do this fast. I pray for strength to be able to finish it in Jesus' name.
2. I thank You O Lord for my life and the gift of salvation.
3. I thank You O Lord for the grace of giving of my tithes and offering. Accept them in the name of Jesus.
4. Lord, I thank you for my family. I pray for the salvation of everyone of them in the name of Jesus.
5. Lord, teach me to thank You everyday for your goodness towards my loved ones and I.

*Notes*_____

_____

_____

_____

_____

_____

_____

Day 31
I SPEAK TO EVERY STORM IN MY LIFE TO BECOME CALM

Scripture: Matthew 8:23-27

23 Now when He got into a boat, His disciples followed Him. 24 And suddenly a great tempest arose on the sea, so that the boat was covered with the waves. But He was asleep. 25 Then His disciples came to Him and awoke Him, saying, "Lord, save us! We are perishing!"

26 But He said to them, "Why are you fearful, O you of little faith?" Then He arose and rebuked the winds and the sea, and there was a great calm. 27 So the men marveled, saying, "Who can this be, that even the winds and the sea obey Him?"

PRAYERS

1. Every furious storm blowing against my life, become calm in the name of Jesus.
2. O God, arise and restore peace and calmness into the ship of my life.
3. Every problem in my life, begin to receive instant solution in the name of Jesus.
4. Lord Jesus, arise and fill my life with signs and wonders everyday.
5. Heavenly Father, I ask for and receive the shield of faith that will help extinguish all flaming arrows of the evil ones in Jesus' name.

*Notes*_____

_____

_____

_____

_____

_____

_____

Day 32
LORD, APPEAR TO ME AND
MAKE ME FRUITFUL

Scripture: Genesis 18:1-15

Then the Lord appeared to him by the terebinth trees of Mamre, as he was sitting in the tent door in the heat of the day. 2 So he lifted his eyes and looked, and behold, three men were standing by him; and when he saw them, he ran from the tent door to meet them, and bowed himself to the ground, 3 and said, "My Lord, if I have now found favor in Your sight, do not pass on by Your servant. 4 Please let a little water be brought, and wash your feet, and rest yourselves under the tree. 5 And I will bring a morsel of bread, that you may refresh your hearts. After that you may pass by, inasmuch as you have come to your servant."
They said, "Do as you have said."

Continue to verses 6-15

PRAYERS

1. Lord, send your angels to visit me today and bless me with mighty miracles.
2. Heavenly Father, release me from every manner of barrenness and make me exceedingly fruitful in the name of Jesus.
3. Reveal your glory to me Lord and enable me to behold it in the name of Jesus.
4. Lord, let today be my appointed day of breakthrough, success and victory.
5. Father, let all the long awaited miracles in my life, come to pass speedily in the name of Jesus.

*Notes*_____

_____

_____

_____

_____

_____

_____

Day 33
FULFILL YOUR PROMISES IN MY LIFE, O LORD

Scripture: Genesis 21:1-7

And the Lord visited Sarah as He had said, and the Lord did for Sarah as He had spoken. 2 For Sarah conceived and bore Abraham a son in his old age, at the set time of which God had spoken to him. 3 And Abraham called the name of his son who was born to him—whom Sarah bore to him—Isaac. 4 Then Abraham circumcised his son Isaac when he was eight days old, as God had commanded him. 5 Now Abraham was one hundred years old when his son Isaac was born to him. 6 And Sarah said, "God has made me laugh, and all who hear will laugh with me." 7 She also said, "Who would have said to Abraham that Sarah would nurse children? For I have borne him a son in his old age."

PRAYERS

1. O Lord, be gracious to me in every area of my life.
2. Father, hasten your word to be fulfilled in my life in the name of Jesus.
3. I receive and speak into existence everything that God has promised to do in my life in the name of Jesus.
4. Lord, bring me laughter concerning every difficult situation in my life and let people around me laugh with me in the name of Jesus.
5. I decree and declare that my light shall rise and shine daily in the name of Jesus.

*Notes*_____

_____

_____

_____

_____

_____

_____

Day 34
O LORD, OPEN MY EYES TO SEE MY BLESSINGS

Scriptures: Genesis 21:8-21

8 So the child grew and was weaned. And Abraham made a great feast on the same day that Isaac was weaned.

9 And Sarah saw the son of Hagar the Egyptian, whom she had borne to Abraham, scoffing. 10 Therefore she said to Abraham, "Cast out this bondwoman and her son; for the son of this bondwoman shall not be heir with my son, namely with Isaac." 11 And the matter was very displeasing in Abraham's sight because of his son.

12 But God said to Abraham, "Do not let it be displeasing in your sight because of the lad or because of your bondwoman. Whatever Sarah has said to you, listen to her voice; for in Isaac your seed shall be called.

Continue to verses 13-21

PRAYERS

1. Father, turn every situation in my life around for my good in the name of Jesus.
2. Lord, turn every test I'm currently going through into instant testimony in the name of Jesus.
3. My Lord and my God, hear my cry for mercy and miracles today.
4. O Lord, open my eyes to see the blessings and divine provisions around me in the name of Jesus.
5. Father, bring me in contact with my divine helpers today wherever I go in the name of Jesus.

*Notes*_____

_____

_____

_____

_____

_____

_____

DAY 35
LIGHT OF GOD, SHINE BRIGHTLY IN MY LIFE

Scripture: John 1:1-18

In the beginning was the Word, and the Word was with God, and the Word was God. 2 He was in the beginning with God. 3 All things were made through Him, and without Him nothing was made that was made. 4 In Him was life, and the life was the light of men. 5 And the light shines in the darkness, and the darkness did not comprehend it.

6 There was a man sent from God, whose name was John. 7 This man came for a witness, to bear witness of the Light, that all through him might believe. 8 He was not that Light, but was sent to bear witness of that Light. 9 That was the true Light which gives light to every man coming into the world.

Continue to verses 10-18

PRAYERS

1. I pray that the light of God shall eliminate every darkness in my life in the name of Jesus.
2. Power, strength and grace of the living God, be multiplied unto me in the name of Jesus.
3. Lord, let every darkness in my home, community and in the city where I live be eliminated in the name of Jesus.
4. Father, reveal Jesus to every lost soul in my community so that they will become saved.
5. Lord, empower me to be able to share my faith boldly everyday in the name of Jesus.

*Notes*_____

_____

_____

_____

_____

_____

Day 36
LAMB OF GOD, REIGN AND RULE IN MY LIFE

Scripture: John 1:19-34

19 Now this is the testimony of John, when the Jews sent priests and Levites from Jerusalem to ask him, "Who are you?"

20 He confessed, and did not deny, but confessed, "I am not the Christ."

21 And they asked him, "What then? Are you Elijah?"

He said, "I am not."

"Are you the Prophet?" And he answered, "No."

22 Then they said to him, "Who are you, that we may give an answer to those who sent us? What do you say about yourself?"

23 He said: "I am The voice of one crying in the wilderness: "Make straight the way of the Lord,""[g] as the prophet Isaiah said."

Continue to verses 24-34

PRAYERS

1. O God, help me to surrender my life to you wholeheartedly each day.
2. I receive the mind of Christ to enable me live a righteous life, pleasing and acceptable unto God.
3. O Lord, make me a true ambassador of Christ wherever I go each day.
4. Spirit of the living God, come upon me afresh today in the name of Jesus.
5. O Lord, give me a powerful testimony of being used for your glory today.
6. Father, reign and rule in the heart of every man of God so that they will all be a blessing to their flocks in Jesus' name.

*Notes*_____

_____

_____

_____

_____

Day 37
PRAISE GOD FOR HIS GOODNESS

Scripture: Psalms 147.

Praise the Lord!
For it is good to sing praises to our God;
For it is pleasant, and praise is beautiful.
2 The Lord builds up Jerusalem;
He gathers together the outcasts of Israel.
3 He heals the brokenhearted
And binds up their wounds.
4 He counts the number of the stars;
He calls them all by name.
5 Great is our Lord, and mighty in power;
His understanding is infinite.
6 The Lord lifts up the humble;
He casts the wicked down to the ground.
7 Sing to the Lord with thanksgiving;
Sing praises on the harp to our God,

Continue to verses 8-20

PRAYERS

1. Lord, as I bring sacrifices of praise and adoration to you this day, accept them in the name of Jesus.
2. Father, show your love and compassion to me in great measure.
3. O Lord, let the kingdom of God be firmly established in my heart, in my home and in the city where I live in the name of Jesus.
4. King of glory, let every word I utter today bring honor and adoration to your holy name in the name of Jesus.
5. Father, let your goodness and greatness be revealed to all flesh today.

*Notes*_____

_____

_____

_____

_____

_____

Day 38
LET HEAVENS AND EARTH PRAISE THE LORD

Scripture: Psalms 148

Praise the Lord!
Praise the Lord from the heavens;
Praise Him in the heights!
2 Praise Him, all His angels;
Praise Him, all His hosts!
3 Praise Him, sun and moon;
Praise Him, all you stars of light!
4 Praise Him, you heavens of heavens,
And you waters above the heavens!
5 Let them praise the name of the Lord,
For He commanded and they were created.
6 He also established them forever and ever;
He made a decree which shall not pass away.
7 Praise the Lord from the earth,
You great sea creatures and all the depths;

Continue to verses 8-14

PRAYERS

1. Lord, let today be a wonderful day of rejoicing for me and my loved ones in Jesus' name.

2. I decree that all the elements and heavenly bodies shall praise the name of the Lord and declare His glory in a special way today.

3. Father, I decree that all the elements, the sun, the moon and the stars shall cooperate with me this day in the name of Jesus.

4. O Lord, let your name be magnified in my life today.

5. I declare that I shall receive a plethora of uncommon miracles today in the name of Jesus.

*Notes*_____

_____

_____

_____

_____

_____

Day 39
O LORD, BRING YOUR WORK
TO COMPLETION IN MY LIFE

Scriptures: Isaiah 61:1-3; Psalms 149

"The Spirit of the Lord God is upon Me,
Because the Lord has anointed Me
To preach good tidings to the poor;
He has sent Me to heal the brokenhearted,
To proclaim liberty to the captives,
And the opening of the prison to those who are bound;
2 To proclaim the acceptable year of the Lord,
And the day of vengeance of our God;
To comfort all who mourn,
3 To console those who mourn in Zion,
To give them beauty for ashes,
The oil of joy for mourning,
The garment of praise for the spirit of heaviness;
That they may be called trees of righteousness,
The planting of the Lord, that He may be glorified."

Further Scripture reading: Psalms 149

PRAYERS

1. Father, give me a surprise of good news that will be of great joy today.
2. Prepare my feet for dancing and my tongue to sing your praises today, O Lord my God.
3. Lord, replace my tears with songs of joy today and everyday in the name of Jesus.
4. Father, restore unto me speedily all my fortunes and prosperity stolen from me in the name of Jesus.
5. Lord, heal every disease and sickness in my body in the name of Jesus.

*Notes*_____

_____

_____

_____

_____

_____

_____

_____

Day 40
PRAISE THE LORD IN YOUR INMOST BEING

Scriptures: Psalms 100 & 150

Make a joyful shout to the Lord, all you lands!
2 Serve the Lord with gladness;
Come before His presence with singing.
3 Know that the Lord, He is God;
It is He who has made us, and not we ourselves;[a]
We are His people and the sheep of His pasture.
4 Enter into His gates with thanksgiving,
And into His courts with praise.
Be thankful to Him, and bless His name.
5 For the Lord is good;
His mercy is everlasting,
And His truth endures to all generations.

Further Scripture reading: Isaiah 61:4-8, Psalms 95, and 150

PRAYERS

1. Father, I praise and bless Your holy name for all the blessings, victories, breakthroughs and restoration released upon me during this 40-day fast.
2. Lord, as I bring my heart of thanksgiving to you this day, accept all of it.
3. I pray that all the miracles God has released upon my life shall endure and be made permanent in the name of Jesus.
4. Lord, I possess permanently the new blessings, breakthroughs, beautification, provisions, healing and extraordinary miracles you have granted me in the name of Jesus.
5. Father, help me to walk upright before you everyday of my life in the name of Jesus. AMEN!

*Notes*_____

_____

_____

_____

_____

ABOUT THE AUTHOR

Dr. Yemi Ebenezer Ajimatanrareje is the founding pastor of Open Heavens Church, in Brentwood, California. He and his wife, Dr. Rose Ajimatanrareje, had previously planted a Church in Miami, Florida in 2002 and helped plant another in Port-au-Prince, Haiti in 2013.

Pastor Yemi studied Mass Communication at the University of Lagos in Nigeria where he obtained his B.S. and M.S. degrees. After receiving his call to preach the gospel in 1999, he resigned from being a manager at Bank of America and enrolled at the Golden Gate Baptist Theological Seminary, San Francisco and graduated with Master's of Divinity. In 2006, he received his Doctor of Ministry degree from Jacksonville Baptist Theological Seminary, Jacksonville, Florida.

Dr. Yemi is a succinct Bible teacher, a marriage counselor, a revivalist and a prayer stalwart. He is the author of *Release for All Captives*.

He and his wife, with their children, reside in Brentwood, California.